VOTING RIGHTS,
VOTING WRONGS

A Twentieth Century Fund Paper

VOTING RIGHTS, VOTING WRONGS

The Legacy of *BAKER v. CARR*

by Bernard Grofman

P̶P Priority Press Publications/New York/1990

The Twentieth Century Fund is a research foundation undertaking timely analyses of economic, political, and social issues. Not-for-profit and nonpartisan, the Fund was founded in 1919 and endowed by Edward A. Filene.

Library of Congress Cataloging-in-Publication Data

Grofman, Bernard.
   Voting rights, voting wrongs: the legacy of Baker v. Carr /
by Bernard Grofman
      p.   cm.
   Includes bibliographical references and index.
   ISBN 0-87078-295-9
   1. Apportionment (Election law)—United States. 2. Election
districts—United States. I. Title
KF4905.G76   1990
342.73'053—dc20
[347.30253]   90-11236
                                                                 CIP

FOREWORD

In 1962, The Twentieth Century Fund sponsored a conference on electoral districts. Those in attendance concluded that "in the light of democratic principles, of history and of contemporary political theory, the only legitimate basis of representation in a state legislature is people. One man's vote must be worth the same as another's." That same year, the United States Supreme Court ruled in *Baker v. Carr* that our Constitution mandated the principle of "one man-one vote." Although *Baker* and its progeny dramatically changed legislative apportionment in this country, a number of constitutional and policy questions remain unresolved.

Consider the intersection of voting rights for minorities and apportionment. For most of our history, laws or threats have conspired to exclude African-Americans from the voting booth and, thereby, political power. In 1965, Congress passed the Voting Rights Act, which began the task of eliminating racial discrimination from elections. As time passed, many experts came to believe that in electoral districts where whites rarely voted for minority candidates, the ballots of minority voters could be construed as counting for little. In response, in 1982, Congress amended the Voting Rights Act to make it more likely that district lines would be drawn to concentrate minority voters, which would, in turn, result in the election of minority candidates. Congress acted to improve the chances that the minorities, in fact, might gain political power.

Race and politics rarely meet in the United States without a chaperon of controversy. The change in the Voting Rights Act is no exception to that rule. Critics have maintained that the alterations will lead to a "resegregation" of American politics that will damage both the interests of minorities and the nation as a whole. Others see the changes as modest steps toward a more pluralistic polity that realizes the political aspirations of minorities.

Unfortunately, the national census has also become a racially charged issue. The Census Bureau acknowledges that certain Americans—especially Hispanics and African-Americans—are less likely to be counted. The consequence, of course, is reduced representation in states where there are large numbers of minorities. What should be done about the undercount? Should the Census Bureau adjust their enumeration to make up for the missing?

Finally, the hoary practice of partisan gerrymandering has become a constitutional issue. Assuming that drawing district lines to favor one party or another is properly a judicial concern, the question must arise whether a sensible and practical remedy can be devised to prevent such gerrymandering.

The Twentieth Century Fund has long been interested in voting and apportionment. The 1962 conference mentioned earlier led to the publication of *One Man-One Vote*, an influential defense of equality in electoral districting. The Fund also supported Robert B. McKay's *Reapportionment: The Law and Politics of Equal Representation*, which appeared in 1965. More recently, Abigail Thernstrom's *Whose Votes Count?* dealt with these questions.

 This paper by Bernard Grofman, a leading expert in the field, treats these questions with knowledge and objectivity. The Fund thanks Grofman for his effort, which we hope will make a constructive contribution to this important debate about the meaning and reality of American democracy.

Richard C. Leone, DIRECTOR
The Twentieth Century Fund
September 1990

CONTENTS

INTRODUCTION

Brown v. Board of Education (1954) and *Baker v. Carr* (1962) are almost universally held to be the two most important decisions of the U.S. Supreme Court in the post–World War II era.[1] The Voting Rights Act of 1965 is almost universally held to be the most successful legislation of the same period. Each addressed a fundamental inequality—segregated education in the case of *Brown*, unequal apportionment in the case of *Baker*, denial of the effective right to vote in the case of the Voting Rights Act. And in each case it was held that remedy of the inequality was within the purview of judicial review and/or administrative action at the federal level. This essay explores representation and redistricting, the issues arising from *Baker v. Carr* and its progeny, and the Voting Rights Act of 1965 and its subsequent amendments and judicial interpretations.

Like almost every major constitutional case, *Baker v. Carr* can be viewed at three levels: (1) an exercise in constitutional interpretation, (2) a dispute about democratic theory, (3) a power struggle. The same is true for the Voting Rights Act of 1965.

Baker and its "one person, one vote" concept is now so much a part of the bedrock of American constitutional law that it is hard to imagine a time when it was controversial. Yet until redistricting changed the landscape of state legislatures and Congress, it was quite probable that judicial intervention in reapportionment would have been permanently blocked by a constitutional amendment proposed by Senator Everett Dirksen of Illinois.

The "one person, one vote" doctrine was challenged by critics on constitutional grounds because attributing this intent to the framers was said to be a historically strained interpretation. However, as Justice Black points out in *Wesberry v. Sanders*, the "Great Compromise" was intended to provide equal representation in the House for equal numbers of people, and even Justice Harlan agreed that the framers expected Congress to use its powers under Article 1, sections 4 and 5, to assure that states would create congressional districts containing substantially equal numbers of people. (Of course, Justice Harlan also believed that *only* Congress and not the courts had the power to remedy congressional malapportionment.) Applications of the "one person, one vote" standard to the states rely on the 14th Amendment.[2] However, the historical evidence is that many states maintained representation in one or both houses of the legislature on a basis other than pure population, and new states were admitted (and southern states readmitted) to the Union with population inequalities in one or both houses. Thus, direct reliance on the 14th Amendment to overturn population inequalities in state legislatures seems to be stretching the historical record. My own view is that population equality, like other aspects of equal protection, can best be viewed in the light of a constitutional jurisprudence that treats the Constitution as a historically evolving document whose interpretation is responsive to contemporary understanding of the fundamental principles of liberty, equality, and democracy. The notion that the Constitution is a "living document," however, was highly controversial in the 1960s and remains somewhat controversial even now, although once-"revisionist" decisions like *Baker* have become sacrosanct.

But the more important source of objection to the Supreme Court's intervention into reapportionment was the dramatic change inaugurated by *Baker* et al. in power relationships. *Baker* was one of a series of events that sealed the doom of a states' rights view of American politics. It asserted unequivocally the supremacy of federal law (and federal courts) over state election practices. While state's rights doctrines had been steadily eroded by historical realities as the role of the federal government steadily grew, *Baker* and subsequent opinions asserted a unified, national view of representation as supreme over state constitutional provisions. More directly, *Baker* signaled the end of rural domination of state politics and of rural overrepresentation in the halls of Congress.

The earlier failure to reapportion was equivalent to gerrymandering. In 1960, the largest district in Tennessee had more than 44 times the population of the smallest district; in California the ratio of the largest to smallest district was 449 to 1.[3] A majority of states had constitutional provisions that assigned legislative representation in whole or in part on some basis other than population. Georgia's unit voting system (roughly speaking, "one county, one legislator") was the most blatant form of gerrymandering, but many states (like California) had restrictions on the maximum number of legislative representatives that populous urban areas could be given. Even in the case of congressional districts, rural districts were less populous than urban ones. As Leroy Hardy aptly put it, legislative resistance to population-based reapportionment was "an attempt to ignore the great transition in American life from a rural to an urban society, 'status quo' elements naturally fought vigorously the realignment of districts which would deplete their political power."[4] Resistance to *Baker* was the last gasp of rural elements who saw America as no longer theirs.

Finally, *Baker* et al. were controversial in terms of democratic theory because these cases rejected the notion that rural interests were entitled to special representation, serving as the bulwark of Jeffersonian democracy (or to put it more crassly as protection against the rootless urban masses), and because they rejected the Burkean view of representation based on permanent interests, not mere numbers.

The Voting Rights Act of 1965 was another watershed in recent American history. Passed by an overwhelming majority, with most southern Democrats in opposition, it is one of the foundations of the "Second Reconstruction." As a result of the act and its subsequent amendments, blacks have gone from virtual exclusion from the politics of the Deep South to positions of authority. (In 1988, thirty-six of eighty-two Democratic county chairmen in Mississippi were black.) Since the mid–1970s, hundreds of cities, counties, and school boards have shifted from at-large election systems to single-member district (SMD) plans as a result of litigation either brought or threatened under the Voting Rights Act. Largely as a result of the act, black and Hispanic representation at the local level in states throughout the South and Southwest has increased dramatically (roughly tripling, for example, in the nearly sixty Texas cities that shifted from at-large to SMD plans).[5]

The widely hailed Voting Rights Act has, however, also been subject to a barrage of criticism. When it was up for renewal in 1982, there were attempts to restrict its scope severely. From a constitutional standpoint, it is attacked because it seeks to extend the Fourteenth Amendment's "equal protection clause" (and Thirteenth Amendment protections against badges of servitude) to cover not merely the right to vote free of harassment or intimidation, but also the right of a protected group (blacks, Hispanics, Asians, Native Americans) to have equal opportunity to participate in the electoral process and to elect candidates of choice. To effectuate this right, federal courts have struck down at-large election systems in jurisdictions where minority electoral success has been minimal and where a single-member district plan could be drawn so that at least one district had a sufficient minority voting population to ensure it "a realistic opportunity to elect candidates of choice." Despite explicit Supreme Court disclaimers to the contrary, critics of the act have charged that this meant reading a nonexistent right to proportional representation into the Constitution.[6]

From the standpoint of democratic theory, the act is attacked because it sets a standard for representation (a) that is based on group rights, not individual rights, (b) that is allegedly based on equality of result, not equality of opportunity, and that effectively requires the creation of constituencies that are racially/linguistically homogeneous as the remedy for the consequences of racially polarized voting patterns rather than relying on political competition and cross-ethnic coalition building *within* electoral constituencies.

From the standpoint of power relationships, like *Baker v. Carr*, the act further asserts the preeminence of the federal government over states and other localities. It even designates certain jurisdictions as having "unclean hands"[7] and gives the Department of Justice (and the District of Columbia Federal District Court) tremendous power over them, effectively denying them the right to change election methods (even such seemingly minor ones as the location of polling booths) without the approval of either the Justice Department or the federal bench. The act has forced hundreds of local jurisdictions to change their form of government.[8]

The following discussion of both *Baker v. Carr* and the Voting Rights Act will focus on the evolution of voting rights case law, especially as it applies to racial and linguistic groups and, more recently, to political parties.

THE EVOLUTION OF VOTING RIGHTS

Introduction

In the landmark *Baker* decision, the Supreme Court held little more than that judicial redress could be sought to compel periodic legislative reapportionment in accord with new census data. In the cases that followed, the lower federal courts (and state courts) held a large number of state legislative reapportionments unconstitutional. In 1963, in the landmark case of *Gray v. Sanders*, Justice William Douglas, speaking for the Court majority, stated in an obiter dictum what was to become the catchphrase of the reapportionment revolution: "one person, one vote." Justice Potter Stewart, in a concurring opinion,[9] used the phrase "one voter, one vote." The phrase "one man, one vote" dates back at least as far as the late nineteenth century in England. It also served as the title of a 1962 Twentieth Century Fund Conference on *Baker v. Carr*.[10] The conference may have been one of the sources for popularization of the phrase.[11] In 1964, in a Georgia congressional case, *Wesberry v. Sanders*,[12] the court held—in language again paralleling that in the Twentieth Century Fund Conference Report—that reapportionment required that "one man's vote . . . is to be worth as much as another's"; in *Reynolds v. Sims*[13] the Court stated that "an individual's right to vote for state legislators is unconstitutionally impaired when its weight is, in a substantial fashion, diluted when compared with votes of citizens living in other parts of the state."

During the next two decades, the Supreme Court established a two-tiered standard. State and local redistricting was constitutional if the total population deviation was under 10 percent, but congressional redistricting plans had to satisfy a much harsher test whereby all possible population deviation among districts was to be eliminated (absent a compelling state purpose that applied uniformly across the state).

The theme of unconstitutional vote dilution is broached in *Reynolds v. Sims,* a progeny of *Baker,* in the context of discrimination against groups identifiable in terms of geography. But in a gerrymander case that predated *Baker* involving the exclusion of blacks from city annexation (*Gomillion v. Lightfoot,*)[14] the principle had already been established that the Constitution forbids a state to draw up districts in a way that deliberately and invidiously discriminates against one class of citizens. Thus, a Court ruling against racial injustice subsequently evolved into a ruling against political inequality. Similarly, without the successful experience of redistricting reforms triggered by *Baker v. Carr,* it seems highly unlikely that there would have been direct intervention of federal courts (and the Justice Department) in state election processes as established in Section 5 of the Voting Rights Act. Without the lessons of *Baker v. Carr,* I believe the Voting Rights Act of 1965 would have emerged a far weaker document in terms of its enforcement mechanisms.[15]

The Voting Rights Act of 1965

The Voting Rights Act of 1965 was intended to provide equal voting rights to blacks. It has been followed, both immediately and in the two decades since, by dramatic growth in black registration and black voter turnout and even more dramatic increases in the number of black elected officials.[16] As amended in 1975 and thereafter, it has also had significant consequences for Hispanic representation and some limited but important consequences for Native American representation in the Southwest, especially since 1982, when voting rights litigation under the newly amended Section 2 of the Voting Rights Act became the normal way to seek redress for vote dilution rather than filing a case directly under the Fourteenth or Fifteenth Amendment.

From a policy perspective the Voting Rights Act has five key components:

(1) 1965 provisions abolishing literacy tests (initially for a given time period, subsequently made a permanent prohibition). This barrier, customarily enforced with a double standard for whites and blacks, was a key part of the post-Reconstruction elimination of black suffrage in the South.[17]

(2) 1965 provisions permitting the Justice Department to dispatch federal marshals as observers in parts of the South to end the denial of voting rights to blacks. The protective cloak of the federal government was especially important in the 1960s when black registration in many areas of the South was virtually nil but harassment and intimidation of blacks seeking to exercise the franchise were commonplace.[18]

(3) 1965 provisions requiring jurisdictions covered by Section 5 to submit *any* proposed change in election provisions at every level of government to the Depart-

ment of Justice for preclearance, to ensure that the proposed change does not have the effect or purpose of abridging minority voting rights. (Initially, these jurisdictions were all in the South, but in 1975 provisions extended to all or part of twenty-two other states, including New York and Colorado. Currently, sixteen states are covered in whole or part by the act.) The preclearance requirement became important in reapportionment during the 1970s, when it led to the substantial elimination of multimember district plans in southern legislatures. Earlier, these districts had been used to submerge pockets of black population that were large enough to form the core of single-member districts. In states such as South Carolina and Mississippi, this change (in conjunction with black registration gains) dramatically increased the number of black legislators.[19]

(4) 1975 provisions that added Hispanics and Asians to the list of protected groups and required the use of bilingual ballots in jurisdictions with sufficient population (greater than 5 percent) whose native language was not English. These provisions have had their primary impact in Hispanic concentrations in both the Northeast and the Southwest.

(5) 1982 amendments (Section 2) that prohibited the use of any electoral device that would have the purpose or effect of diluting minority voting strength. Section 5 preclearance requirements affected only *changes* in election procedures, meaning discriminatory practices could continue even if they could not be initiated. Section 5, moreover, affected only some states, and, prior to 1982, the decisions were under constitutional standards rather than under the "results" stan-

dard of Section 2. Although amended Section 2 provisions did not have the prohibitory power of Section 5 preclearance requirements, they were potentially of far greater importance—especially in ending the discriminatory use of at-large elections. In 1980, over 60 percent of all U.S. cities elected some, and usually all, of their council members at large.[20] It is one of the best-substantiated propositions in political science that in jurisdictions with big (but not preponderant) minority populations, at-large elections tend to depress levels of minority electoral success.[21]

*   *   *

In the 1960s, the most important provisions of the Voting Rights Act were seen as those dealing with protecting the rights of southern blacks to register and vote. In the 1970s, Hispanics and other minority groups were included in the act, and the Section 5 preclearance provisions were considered of primary significance. After the 1982 amendments, the new language of Section 2 became the basis of most voting rights lawsuits. As with the decisions in *Brown* and *Baker,* it has taken almost two decades for the full scope and consequences of the Voting Rights Act to become clear.

Political Gerrymandering

In *Reynolds v. Sims* the Supreme Court enunciated a justification for its involvement in redistricting: the need to guarantee "fair and effective representation."[22] By defining quality of representation in terms of equally populated districts, the Supreme Court was able to avoid coming to grips with more fundamental issues such as the constitutionality of at-large elections and the meaning of minority vote dilution. In the area of racial representation, however, in cases such as *White v. Regester* and *Rogers v. Lodge,* the Court was forced to address these questions.[23]

Intentional racial gerrymandering has been held to be prohibited by the Fourteenth and Fifteenth amendments (see, for example, *Gomillion v. Lightfoot* and *Rogers v. Lodge*), and districting that has the effect of diluting black, Hispanic, Asian, or Native American voting strength is prohibited by the 1982 amendments to Section 2 of the Voting Rights Act.[24] But political gerrymandering was not held to be justiciable in the two decades since *Baker v. Carr.* Throughout the 1960s and 1970s, federal courts held political gerrymandering in single-member districts to be nonjusticiable, although the door was left open for possible litigation in *multi*member districts.

A 1983 case before the Supreme Court suggested that the legal status of political gerrymandering might be about to change. Various opinions in *Karcher v. Daggett,*[25] a suit challenging population discrepancies in New Jersey's congressional districts, indicated that a number of Supreme Court justices had come to believe that reliance on a numerical "one person, one vote" standard could not guarantee the "fair and effective representation" whose achievement was arguably the justification for the Court's intervention in redistricting in the first place. Indeed, Justice John Paul Stevens's concurring opinion in *Karcher,* and Justice Lewis F. Powell, Jr.'s separate dissenting opinion, argued explicitly for the desirability of judicial review of political gerrymandering. In particular, Justice Stevens had provided a detailed discussion of appropriate criteria to test for signs of intentional political maneuvering. Many scholars (myself included) believed that as of 1983 there were at least five potential votes on the Court in favor of the justiciability of the issue.

Two suits were brought in federal district courts in the 1980s challenging state or congressional districting plans on political gerrymandering grounds, one brought by Republicans in a state controlled by Democrats (California, *Badham v. Eu*),[26] and one brought by Democrats in a state controlled by Republicans (Indiana, *Bandemer v. Davis*). *Bandemer* was decided in favor of the Democratic plaintiffs in 1984 and was reviewed on appeal (under the name *Davis v. Bandemer*) by the Supreme Court in June 1986. *Badham* was dismissed in 1988 by a federal district court, a dismissal affirmed per curiam by the Supreme Court.

The district court majority in *Bandemer* was largely guided by the views of Justice Stevens in his concurring opinion in *Karcher*. Justice Stevens enunciated three elements that a claim of unconstitutional gerrymandering must satisfy before being considered justiciable. Plaintiffs must provide:

(1) a demonstration that they "belong to a politically salient class . . . whose geographical distribution is sufficiently ascertainable that it could have been taken into account into drawing district boundaries";

(2) a demonstration that "in relevant district or districts or in the state as a whole, their proportionate voting influence has been adversely affected by the challenged scheme";

(3) "a prima facie showing that raises a rebuttable presumption of discrimination."[27]

By a two-to-one majority, the *Bandemer* court held that this threefold test had been met. It found that the defendants had failed to provide acceptable justifications for deviations from compactness (which the court regarded as severe) and asserted that the districts, especially those in the House, were drawn with "little apparent emphasis on 'community of interest.'" Also, the plan's origins were characterized as "fiercely competitive and unashamedly partisan," and the majority party was held to have been motivated to "insulate itself from risk of losing control of the General Assembly."[28]

Perhaps the most controversial element of the *Bandemer* majority's reasons, other than the very fact that for the first time political gerrymandering was clearly held to be justiciable, was its reliance on a measure of the discrepancy between the vote share received by the Democrats and their share of legislative seats as a direct measure of the impact of gerrymandering: in the Indiana House, 51.9 percent of the statewide votes for house members, but only 43 percent of the (one hundred) seats; in the Indiana Senate, 53.1 percent of the statewide votes for state senators but only 52.0 percent of the seats up for election in that year. The dissenting judge asserted that "a comparison between the percentage of Democratic votes cast statewide for legislative candidates and the number of seats actually won, standing alone, fails to prove dilution."[29] He recalculated the seats-vote discrepancy, using a methodology that he claimed was supported by the expert opinion cited by Justice Stevens in *Karcher*.[30] Using that methodology, the proper baseline of Democratic strength was 46 percent of the votes, not 51.9 percent. The comparison of 46 percent of the votes with 43 percent of the seats failed to demonstrate that plaintiffs have suffered vote dilution.[31] Moreover, in the Indiana Senate, with only twenty-five seats being contested, 52.0 percent (thirteen seats) was as close to perfect proportionality with 53.2 percent of the votes as could mathematically be achieved.

When *Bandemer* was heard on appeal by the U.S. Supreme Court (under the name *Davis v. Bandemer*), the Supreme Court upheld the justiciability of political gerrymandering but reversed the lower court's finding that the Indiana plans were an unconstitutional gerrymander. However, there was no majority opinion in *Davis v. Bandemer*. Moreover, the puzzling failure of the Supreme Court to hear *Badham v. Eu* on its merits means that the probability of court action to prevent political gerrymandering is highly uncertain as we enter the 1990s.

ISSUES OF THE 1990s

Outstanding Issues—An Overview

Baker v. Carr and the amended Voting Rights Act of 1965 have dramatically changed the nature of U.S. redistricting practices at all levels of government. Nonetheless, a number of critical constitutional and policy questions with respect to voting rights and vote dilution remain unresolved. Like *Brown v. Board of Education,* both *Baker v. Carr* and the Voting Rights Act were highly controversial at the outset but have since come to be regarded as fundamental bulwarks of liberty, even as subsequent decisions remain controversial (for example, busing to remedy segregated schools, absurdly precise standards of population equality in redistricting, overruling local choices of election methods).

Currently, the two most important controversies are standards for determining vote dilution for racial and linguistic minorities in the context of the Voting Rights Act and standards for determining when partisan gerrymandering rises to the level of a constitutional violation. Each issue raises several key questions.

Major questions concerning the Voting Rights Act include:

(1) Should minority vote dilution be judged on whether minorities have an "equal opportunity to elect candi-

dates of choice," or only on whether they have been denied the franchise or other means of access to the political system? If the former, is this a proportional representation standard in disguise, as some critics have claimed?

(2) Has the new (1982) language of Section 2 of the Voting Rights Act led to a "resegregation" of American politics, as Abigail Thernstrom[32] and other critics have claimed, or rather, have the new provisions led to a revitalization of American pluralistic politics by opening the possibility of electoral success to groups previously largely shut out of the political process?

(3) For purposes of apportionment (for example, of congressional seats to the states), should there be a statistical adjustment for the undercount of Hispanics, blacks, and other minorities known to have occurred in previous decennial census enumerations? If so, how should that adjustment be made? Conversely, should noncitizens be counted at all in the population figures used for reapportionment and districting?

The issues concerning political gerrymandering include:

(4) Was it a mistake for the Supreme Court (in *Davis v. Bandemer*) to have declared partisan gerrymandering to be justiciable?

(5) Does the standard in *Davis v. Bandemer,* which requires evidence of "continued frustration of the will of a majority of the voters or effective denial to a minority of voters of a fair chance to influence the

political process"[33] for a plan to be held unconstitutional, provide courts with sufficiently clear guidelines to permit expeditious resolution of political gerrymandering claims without bogging courts down in a quagmire?

(6) Should redistricting be left to legislatures, or should it be taken out of legislative hands and entrusted to a bipartisan (or so-called nonpartisan) commission? If districting is to be left to legislatures, are there ways to mitigate the worst forms of gerrymandering, for example, by imposing strict formal standards of compactness, or by requiring supramajoritarian (or bipartisan) consensus?

(7) What will be the consequences of *Bandemer* for redistricting in the 1990s?

(8) Has the Supreme Court carried its insistence on exact numerical equality of population to the level of *reductio ad absurdum,* and in the process lost sight of the ideal of "fair and effective" representation?

Issues and Answers

Criteria for minority vote dilution. The single most important thing that happened to minority voting rights in the 1980s is that the amended Section 2 of the Voting Rights Act made a showing of discriminatory effects sufficient to find a violation, even without proof of intentional discrimination. This effectively mooted the Supreme Court decision in *Mobile v. Bolden.*[34] The new language made it easier for minority groups to replace at-large elections with single-member districts in jurisdictions where racially polarized voting led their voting strength to be submerged by the white majority. It tends to be easier to prove that an at-large plan has had a discriminatory effect than that it had a discriminatory purpose. Given contemporary U.S. political realities, in areas with sufficient minority population to form a (majority) minority single-member district but where whites form the overall majority, a discriminatory effect of at-large elections is likely.[35]

The second most important thing that happened concerning racial vote dilution is that the Supreme Court in *Thornburg v. Gingles* dramatically simplified the previous, multifaceted, "totality of circumstances" effects test for vote dilution in at-large or multimember district elections used by courts prior to 1982 and replaced it with a simple, three-pronged test under the new Section 2: (1) Can a (majority) minority single-member district be drawn? (2) Is voting racially polarized? (3) Is the level of white crossover voting so low that minority candidates usually lose?

The third most important development is that the Department of Justice under President Reagan, although generally quite hostile to the Voting Rights Act, continued the use of Section 5 preclearance denial (or threat thereof) to rule out continuing use of multimember districts by southern state legislatures. Thus, in state legislative districting, in areas of substantial minority population, single-member districts are now the norm.[36]

The fourth important event in the evolution of voting rights law is the increasing role of civil rights organizations such as the NAACP, the NAACP Legal Defense and Educational Fund, the Mexican American Legal Defense and Educational Fund, the Southwest Voter Registration and Education Project, the Lawyers' Committee for Civil Rights Under Law, and the American Civil Liberties Union. These organizations have had a remarkable record of success in litigating the elimination of at-large elections in cities, counties, and school boards with a substantial minority population that had achieved only minimal representation under the at-large plan. The recent success rate for such suits against Texas cities, to cite one example, is about 95 percent.[37]

The new language of Section 2 of the Voting Rights Act, the Supreme Court's interpretation of that language, and the aggressive litigation strategy pursued by minority groups against use of at-large elections in areas of substantial minority population continued a trend begun in the 1970s. Arguably, the choices being made in the 1980s were choices among competing theories of representation. However, it is a mistake to claim (as does Thernstrom)[38] that the Section 2 test is equivalent to a requirement of proportional representation (or at least as near to it as practicable). Single-member district plans will not generally yield proportional representation for minorities.[39] They can produce a dramatic improvement in minority representation over a previous at-large or multimember district system,[40] but they will approximate proportionality only if minority population is highly ghettoized.

Under current case law minority vote dilution is not to be regarded solely as a problem of access to the ballot free of intimidation or vote fraud. Instead, deciding whether there has been minority vote dilution becomes a complex problem involving issues such as choice among type of election system and statistical questions such as thresholds for legally significant levels of racially polarized voting.

Consequences of the Voting Rights Act. The Voting Rights Act raises important policy questions. It has been widely praised for its contributions to the realization of political equality; it has also been criticized as leading to "resegregation" because recent litigation under the act has led to the creation of black-majority districts. Abigail Thernstrom is among the most vocal of critics:

> The Voting Rights Act was 20 years old on August 5 and by now its apple pie aura is camouflage. The right to vote no longer means the right to go into a polling booth and pull the lever. . . . Today an alleged voting rights violation is a districting plan that contains nine majority-black districts when a tenth could be drawn. The question is thus: to how much special protection from white competition are black candidates entitled? When a different plan might give a seat to another black, should the interests of white incumbents give way to the goal of minority office-holding? Are there costs to blacks when a single seat is gained but more widespread influence is lost?

In her recent book, Thernstrom complains that "no amount of argument can persuade the Justice Department that it is legitimate to divide black voters between districts in order to protect a white liberal incumbent who has served the black community well. . . ."[41]

In addition, enthusiasm for the Voting Rights Act has been mitigated by charges that the election of black officials has led to only minimal changes in the social and economic conditions of blacks.[42]

These are serious claims that deserve careful attention. The thrust of Thernstrom's criticism is that remedies (for the paucity of minority officeholders) that involve the creation of single-member districts are bad law, and that they are prime examples of the unintended consequences of legislative behavior. Mack Jones, too, believes that the consequences of the Voting Rights Act are quite different from those intended by its framers, although the basis for his judgment is different from Thernstrom's. Jones holds that the goal of the act's framers—the universal right to cast a ballot—has not provided minorities with the leverage to change their unequal social and economic situation, even in cases in which minority officeholders have won office. Other opponents assert that current trends in vote-dilution litigation under the act will lead to the political "ghetto-ization" of minority groups.

My view is that Jones has unrealistic expectations about what can be achieved by representation alone, and Thernstrom fails to understand that the Voting Rights Act has made possible a genuine pluralist politics at the state and local levels. Before the Voting Rights Act, the magnitude of racially polarized voting in many jurisdictions throughout the United States (using at-large elections) made it all but impossible for minorities to elect candidates of choice, who were themselves members of the minority community, or else prevented minorities from obtaining more than "token" representation.[43] Moreover, the notion that minority populations should be fragmented in order to guarantee the election or reelection of liberals who are not members of the minority community perpetuates a kind of paternalism.

In my view, the Voting Rights Act has been a remarkable success.

Census undercount of minorities and census inclusion of noncitizens. The Census Bureau has acknowledged that certain minorities (notably blacks and Hispanics) are less likely to be enumerated during the decennial census headcount than the population as a whole. Although there is no agreement on the magnitude of the undercount, the general error in 1980 census data is commonly taken to be between 1 and 2 percent, and the undercount of minorities roughly 5 to 6 percent, although the figure may be considerably larger in urban, low-income areas. Because minority population in the United States is not randomly distributed, either within states (it is primarily urban) or across states (black population is heavily concentrated in roughly fifteen states and Hispanic population in five), the minority undercount has been a matter of considerable political concern.

Primarily, the minority undercount affects apportionment at both the national level (in the form of assignment of congressional seats to states on the basis of their population) and at the state level (urban versus suburban versus rural). In addition, population figures are used to determine funding levels to state and local jurisdictions under a variety of federal and state programs. Reliable estimates of minority populations are also politically important in terms of the potential "clout" that each group is seen to have. And finally, public policy decisions on societal needs for various types of human services rely on accurate estimates of the populations that will require the use of those services.

Since the 1980 census, the Census Bureau has been considering ways to deal with minority undercount. Demographers, geographers, and statisticians (both from within the Census Bureau and from the academic community at large) have engaged in a search for alternatives. One controversial proposal (that has a considerable degree of support from the minority community, and from some leading statisticians) is to make use of statistical techniques to "adjust" the census head-count figures to reflect the probable magnitude of the undercount, based on a "post-enumeration follow-up survey."

The controversy is over the significance of creating adjusted census figures that do not reflect "actual bodies" (although some statistical adjustments already take place for households known to exist but for which census forms have not been completed), and there is dispute as to the feasibility of developing a statistical adjustment procedure that will not be successfully challenged in the courts by jurisdictions unhappy with the outcome. Also, it is likely that the "adjusted" figures would not be available until some time after the initial Census Bureau report, or, at best, that they would be quickly available only for the larger units of political geography but not for the small building blocks needed for legislative districting. Thus, there would be two sets of "official" census figures, and because of redistricting deadlines in many state constitutions, it is likely that some jurisdictions would make use of the unadjusted figures for 1990 redistricting.

In October 1987, the Census Bureau announced that it would not attempt a statistical correction for the minority undercount, but would instead improve its enumeration procedures in order to reduce the magnitude of the undercount, even if it did not eliminate it entirely. Some newspaper editorials criticized the decision as a blatantly political one because minorities are more likely to vote for the Democratic party,[44] and Barbara Bailar, associate director for statistical standards of the Census Bureau, resigned from the bureau to protest the decision.[45] House Census subcommittee chairman Mervyn Dymally introduced legislation to reverse the decision prior to the 1990 census, and similar legislation was introduced by Senator Daniel Moynihan of New York. Support comes from such states as California and New York, which would expect to gain additional congressional seats if minority populations are fully counted.

Regardless of the fate of the Dymally or Moynihan legislation, the accuracy of 1990 census figures will be a target of litigation in the 1990s.[46] After the 1980 census, around

fifty lawsuits were filed against the Bureau of the Census
by various states and political subdivisions. Perhaps the
most important of these lawsuits was *Carey v. Klutznick*,[47]
in which the district court held against the bureau and
found (1) that there were statistical adjustments available
that would produce more accurate census counts and (2)
that the Census Bureau is required to use them. However,
this case was reversed on appeal,[48] and certiorari was denied by the Supreme Court.[49]

While I share the view that the Constitution would not
prohibit statistical adjustments of population,[50] as a life-
long Democrat I can attest that there are strong reasons
other than pro-Republican partisanship that lead to opposition to the proposed undercount adjustment. I foresee
a litigation nightmare were the Census Bureau to engage
in substantial statistical adjustments for minority undercount.

As part of a 1990 consent decree in *City of New York
et al. v. Department of Commerce et al.*, civ. 3474 (Eastern
Dist. of N.Y., filed November 3, 1988), the Census Bureau
reversed its previous flat decision to reject statistical adjustment. It agreed to "promptly develop and adopt guidelines articulating . . . relevant technical and nontechnical
statistical and policy grounds for decision on whether to
adjust the 1990 Decennial population counts." These guidelines were submitted for public comment. Nonbinding
recommendation about how to deal with the undercount
will also come from eight experts, four selected by the
government and four named by plaintiffs' attorney. In July
and August of 1990, the Bureau of the Census is conduct-
ing a post-enumeration survey of at least 150,000 units that
will try to measure the undercount for various demograph-
ic and geographic strata. A final decision on undercount
will be made no later than July 15, 1991.

In addition to the unavailability of timely, "corrected" data, the reliance on the post-enumeration census introduces new types of errors into the count as well as the certainty that "attributed" figures will differ from those that can be directly observed. Moreover, even if Bailar is correct that "there is a very broad consensus" in the statistical community "that adjustment would improve the count and decrease the differential,"[51] there will certainly be at least some distinguished statisticians who will testify that, on balance, census adjustment procedures cause more harm than benefit, and/or that the result of applying a national method of adjustment is inappropriate for some given jurisdiction because of special local circumstances.[52]

*   *   *

The Census Bureau is between a rock and a hard place. On the one hand it is being asked to increase the count of minorities by statistical means; on the other hand it is being asked to delete noncitizens from its count.

Should noncitizens be included in the census figures for redistricting? This is an extremely controversial question. There are policy arguments on both sides.[53] If noncitizens are to receive state services (and they often do), ought not redistricting to reflect their presence? After all, six-year-olds cannot vote, but they still are counted for redistricting purposes. On the other hand, why should those who are not part of a community be counted in determining the basis for political representation in that community? For 1980, a not unreasonable estimate of the effects of including noncitizens for purposes of congressional apportionment was that New York and California each gained a seat (and Indiana and Georgia each lost one).

For the case of congressional apportionment, however, it might seem that the answer should be that noncitizens certainly should be counted—the Constitution says that the whole number of "persons" is to be counted. However, even that language is ambiguous and, historically, for example, foreign visitors are excluded from the count. In 1980, a three-judge federal district court in *Federation for American Immigration Reform (FAIR) v. Klutznick*[54] upheld the inclusion of noncitizens in the census count, and this decision was affirmed on appeal, with the Supreme Court denying certiorari. However, the issue is far from resolved, even though another FAIR lawsuit, joined by the states of Kansas and Pennsylvania and by numerous individual members of Congress from around the country, has been dismissed by a federal court for want of standing to sue absent a clear showing of foreseeable harm.[55] Once the census results are out, other lawsuits can be expected.

For state legislative redistricting, the propriety of excluding aliens is less clear. State constitutions differ widely in their provisions as to who is to be counted for apportionment purposes—many exclude Indians not taxed (although this clause is no longer relevant) or soldiers or sailors billeted in the state.[56] Although many state apportionment provisions (for example, those using some nonpopulation-based method such as Georgia's county-unit scheme, or even those using voter registration rather than population as the basis of apportionment) have been struck down as being in violation of "one person, one vote" guidelines, the exclusion of aliens from the state and local apportionments has not to my knowledge ever arisen as an issue. If it became one, a challenge to alien exclusion under the new (1982) language of Section 2 of the Voting Rights Act might be expected. It is possible that provisions excluding noncitizens solely for the purpose of state and local apportionment would not be held unconstitutional.

There is also a practical question. If census figures are

the basis for apportionment, and if those figures do not separate citizens and noncitizens, how can states be given a choice of whether or not to include noncitizens? In previous census years, population data that excluded noncitizens were either unavailable from the Census Bureau at the level of the small-scale geographic units needed for redistricting or were available only too late to do any good. That situation will not change in the 1990 census. Thus, how to deal with noncitizen population in post–1990 redistricting is likely to be an important issue.

Should political gerrymandering be unconstitutional? Analysts who agree with the Supreme Court ruling that political gerrymandering is in violation of the Equal Protection clause of the Fourteenth Amendment (*Bandemer v. Davis,* heard *sub nom Davis v. Bandemer*) believe that eliminating blatant political gerrymandering is necessary to achieve the "fair and effective representation" objective articulated in *Reynolds v. Sims.* However, skeptics (and there are many) believe that there are no manageable standards by which a court can distinguish an unconstitutional gerrymander from "politics as usual," or that the involvement of federal courts in partisan gerrymandering questions will provide an unavoidable political taint to legal judgments. In *Davis v. Bandemer* the Supreme Court reversed (6–3) the district court's (2–1) findings that Indiana's State Senate and State House were unconstitutional gerrymanders, but there was no *majority* consensus on the Supreme Court as to what were the appropriate standards by which partisan gerrymandering was to be judged.

Cynics have already begun to match judges' rulings in political gerrymandering cases with the partisan identification of the president who appointed them to the federal bench, and to claim that judicial decisions in this area may merely be reflections of a barely disguised partisanship. However, I believe that the evidence for this claim is impressionistic and selective.

Clear and manageable standards. While there was no Supreme Court majority consensus in *Bandemer*, there was a plurality opinion written by Justice Byron R. White (joined by three other justices), which in my view (although not in the view of many other scholars) lays out a clear, threefold test for gerrymandering. As I see it, that test requires political gerrymandering to be (1) intentional, (2) predictably nontransient in its effects, and (3) severe in its consequences for representation if it is to be held unconstitutional.

The appropriate indicia for gerrymandering *intent* are not particularly controversial. The Supreme Court treated it here as relatively nonproblematic.[57]

To ascertain whether its *effects* are severe and predictably nontransient, a number of approaches have been suggested. Among the most important of these are (a) the baseline voting strength approach, (b) the seats-votes approach, and (c) the simulation approach.

The political fairness of districting plans can be judged by *baseline measures* of partisan voting strength based on statewide contests.[58] The partisan consequences can also be judged in terms of the plan's expected responsiveness to change in partisan support and analysis of the symmetry with which it treats that support when votes are translated into seats. This approach, commonly know as the *seats-votes approach,* is associated with the work of Richard Niemi of the University of Rochester and his colleagues.[59] Its utility has been challenged by Bruce Cain of the California Institute of Technology.[60]

A third approach involves analysis of the expected fairness of districting plans through use of computer simulation techniques that generate numerous hypothetical plans for comparison purposes.[61] In my view, it is possible to use these tools to make reliable projections about a redistricting plan's probable partisan consequences, especially if that plan has a large number of noncompetitive seats.[62]

The first major case to be decided since *Bandemer, Badham v. Eu,* dismissed (2–1) a Republican challenge to Democrat-drawn congressional plans in California as without merit because they did not rise to the level of a constitutional violation. The district court majority in *Badham* asserted that, since Republicans held 40 percent of California's congressional seats and there is a Republican governor and a Republican U.S. senator ("and given also that a recent former Republican governor of California has for seven years been President of the United States"), "we see the fulcrum of political power to be such as to belie any attempt to plaintiffs to claim that they are bereft of the ability to exercise potent power in 'the political process as a whole' because of the paralysis of an unfair gerrymander."[63] The Supreme Court refused to grant certiorari. The district court decision, which draws almost verbatim from the Democratic congressional delegation pleadings in the case, is, however, of limited precedential value because of the absence of a Supreme Court hearing of the case on the merits.

Proposals to inhibit gerrymandering. One approach to eliminating or reducing gerrymandering is through statutory or state constitutional provisions that strictly implement formal criteria such as compactness, equal population, and maintenance of the integrity of political subunits. (This approach is advocated by public interest organizations such as Common Cause; its leading spokesman over the past two decades has been David Wells of the ILGWU.) A related approach proposes congressional legislation to set guidelines on congressional districting that might reverse or limit some Supreme Court decisions on the need for exact population equality. The idea would be to permit plans that preserved county or city boundaries, making it harder to gerrymander.

Another way to reform the districting process is to remove reapportionment from legislative purview and place it in the hands of an "independent" or "bipartisan" commission, usually with a strict set of formal guidelines of constraints.[64] (This approach, too, is associated with public interest groups such as the League of Women Voters, which implemented such a change in Colorado in the early 1970s.) Based on my reading of the evidence, I am somewhat skeptical about this approach. I believe districting is inherently political. In my view, the notion of blindfolded districting, paying no attention to political outcome but instead looking only at formal guidelines such as compactness or equal population, is fundamentally misguided.[65]

An alternative reform has recently been proposed by Bruce Cain,[66] who has argued for a two-thirds requirement for passage of redistricting plan by a legislature. Such a requirement, Cain argues, would lead to bipartisan compromise and eliminate the most egregious aspects of partisan gerrymandering. Cain's suggestion has considerable merit, provided we recognize that its real effect will simply be a bipartisan, "incumbency preservation" type of gerrymander. This idea was incorporated into an unsuccessful reapportionment initiative in California (Proposition 118, June 1990).

Implications of *Bandemer v. Davis.* I believe that, when legislatures are controlled by what David Mayhew has aptly called "partisan lust,"[67] it is both appropriate and necessary for courts to assure effective representation for all citizens. Nonetheless, if courts are not to be bogged down in a morass of trivial allegations about political unfairness, it is necessary to demand that only gerrymanders whose consequences will be both severe and long-lasting be eligible for challenge. In my view, this is exactly what the Supreme Court has done in its controversial ruling in *Bandemer v. Davis* that political gerrymandering was justiciable but that the lower court erred in finding that the flaws in the 1982 Indiana legislative plans rose to the level of a violation of the Equal Protection clause of the Constitution. This ruling has subsequently been almost completely misinterpreted by the district court majority in *Badham*.

I believe that the practical consequences of the *Bandemer* decision have been significantly overstated by both its opponents and supporters. I have argued elsewhere[68] that egregious *partisan* gerrymandering is far less common than is supposed by the news media, while equally egregious (but not, at least as yet, unconstitutional) *bipartisan* gerrymandering is in fact the norm.[69] It is especially unfortunate in my view that *Badham* was never heard on the merits. California congressional districting, especially in its treatment of former Republican incumbents, presents such blatant facts that the Supreme Court could have struck down the plans drawn by the late congressman Philip Burton while still maintaining a sufficiently high threshold for unconstitutional gerrymandering to avoid an overload of the judicial system.[70]

A mechanical emphasis on population equality. In *Reynolds v. Sims*[71] the Supreme Court set forth the goal of "fair and effective representation" as implicit justification for its involvement in the redistricting process. However, in *Reynolds* as well as in subsequent "one person, one vote" cases, the view shared by most scholars is that the cases lost sight of fair and effective representation. Instead, most analysts believe that the Supreme Court rulings make use of an unduly mechanical insistence on strict standards of population equality, especially for congressional redistricting.[72] In particular, in *Karcher v. Daggett* the Supreme Court repudiated as unacceptable a population deviation that was well within the limits of accuracy of the population counts of the census itself—an average deviation of only 0.14 percent and a total deviation of only 0.69 percent. Moreover, for Congress, differences between states in the size of congressional districts are often very large because of the "rounding off" of the apportionment of congressional seats to each of the states, and because of the constitutional requirement that each state have at least one representative regardless of the state's population. Nevada and Maine, for example, each had the same number of congressmen in 1982 (two), but Nevada's districts averaged 393,345 in population, while those in Maine averaged 562,330. South Dakota, a single-district state, had a congressional seat with a population of 690,178—nearly twice the size of the districts in Nevada.

To remedy the Supreme Court's unduly rigid insistence on exact population equality of congressional districts, I would propose that Congress reassert its own right to set equal population standards for congressional districting— say, a maximum total deviation of 5 percent.

NOTES

1. *Baker v. Carr*, 369 U.S. 186 (1962).

2. Carl A. Auerbach, "The Reapportionment Cases: One Person, One Vote—One Vote, One Value," in *Supreme Court Review*, ed. Philip Kurland (Chicago: University of Chicago Press, 1964). Also see Rosemarie Zagarri, *The Politics of Size: Representation in the United States, 1776–1850* (Ithaca, N.Y.: Cornell University Press, 1987).

3. Leroy C. Hardy, "Considering the Gerrymander," *Pepperdine Law Review* 4 (Spring 1977): 243-84.

4. Ibid., p. 250.

5. Robert Brischetto and Richard Grofman, "Election System, the Voting Rights Act and Minority Representation in Texas Cities and School Boards" (paper presented to the Annual Meeting of the American Political Science Association, Chicago, September 3-6, 1987).

6. See, for example, Abigail Thernstrom, "Voting Rights' Trap," *New Republic* 139, no. 10 (1985): 21-23; and Abigail Thernstrom, *Whose Votes Count? Affirmative Action and Minority Voting Rights* (Cambridge, Mass.: Harvard University Press, 1987).

7. Section 5 preclearance provisions.

8. Brischetto and Grofman, "Election System, the Voting Rights Act and Minority Representation."

9. *Gray v. Sanders*, 372 U.S. 368 at 381 (1963).

10. *One Man, One Vote* (New York: The Twentieth Century Fund, 1962).

11. Robert G. Dixon Jr., *Democratic Representations and Reapportionment in Law and Politics* (New York: Oxford

University Press, 1968), explicitly credits the conference as a mode of transmission.

12. *Wesberry v. Sanders*, 377 U.S. 1 at 8 (1964).

13. *Reynolds v. Sims*, 377 U.S. 533 at 5 (1964).

14. *Gomillion v. Lightfoot*, 364 U.S. 339 (1960).

15. In like manner, without the history of litigation under the Voting Rights Act of 1965, I think it inconceivable that the amendment protection would have subsequently been extended to political parties in *Davis v. Bandemer*, 106 S.Ct. 2797 (1986).

16. *Roster of Black Elected Officials* (Washington: Joint Center for Political Studies, 1976–86).

17. J. Morgan Kousser, "The Undermining of the First Reconstruction," in *Minority Vote Dilution*, ed. Chandler Davidson (Washington, D.C.: Howard University Press, 1984).

18. Steven F. Lawson, *In Pursuit of Power: Southern Blacks and Electoral Politics, 1965–1982* (New York: Columbia University Press, 1985).

19. Bernard Grofman, Michael Migalski, and Nicholas Noviello, "The 'Totality of Circumstances' Test in Section 2 of the Voting Rights Act: A Social Science Perspective," *Law and Policy* 7, no.2 (1985): 209-23.

20. Bernard Grofman, "Alternatives to Single-member Plurality Districts: Legal and Empirical Issues," *Policy Studies Journal 9*, special issue no. 3 (1982): 875-98. Reprinted in *Representation and Redistricting Issues,* ed. Bernard Grofman et al. (Lexington, Mass.: Lexington Books, 1982).

21. Chandler Davidson and George Korbel, "At-Large Elections and Minority-Group Representation: A Re-Examination of Historical and Contemporary Evidence," *Journal of Politics* 43, no. 4 (1981): 983-1005; Grofman, "Alternatives to Single-member Plurality Districts"; Peggy Heilig and Robert J. Mundt, "Do Districts Make a Difference?" *Urban Interest* (April 1981): 62-75; Peggy Heilig and Robert J. Mundt, "Changes in Representational Equity: The Effect of Adopting Districts," *Social Science Quarterly* 64 (June 1983): 393-97; Albert K. Karnig and Susan Welch, *Black Representation and Urban Policy* (Chicago: University

of Chicago Press, 1981), rev. by Dale Rogers Marshall, *American Political Science Review* 75, no. 4 (1981): 1046-47; Richard L. Engstrom and Michael D. McDonald, "The Election of Blacks to City Councils: Clarifying the Impact of Electoral Arrangements on the Seats/Population Relationship," *American Political Science Review* 75, no. 2 (1981): 344-54; Richard L. Engstrom and Michael D. McDonald, "Quantitative Evidence in Vote Dilution Litigation, Part II: Minority Coalitions and Multivariate Analysis," *Urban Lawyer* 19, no. 1 (Winter 1987): 65-75; Richard L. Engstrom and Michael D. McDonald, "The Underrepresentation of Blacks on City Councils: Comparing the Structural and Socioeconomic Explanations for South/Non-South Differences," *Journal of Politics* 44 (1982): 1088-99.

22. *Reynolds v. Sims*, at 565-566.

23. *White v. Regester*, 412 U.S. 755 (1973); *Rogers v. Lodge*, 458 U.S. 613 (1982).

24. *Thornburg v. Gingles*, 105 S.Ct. 2137 (1985).

25. *Karcher v. Daggett*, 462 U.S. 725 (1983).

26. *Badham v. Eu*, no. C-83-1126-RHS (appeal to the Supreme Court filed April 2, 1988).

27. *Karcher v. Daggett*, at 2672.

28. *Bandemer v. Davis*, 603 S. Supp. at 1484.

29. Ibid., at 1501.

30. Charles Backstrom, Leonard Robins, and Scott Eller, "Issues in Gerrymandering: An Exploratory Measure of Partisan Gerrymandering Applied to Minnesota," *Minnesota Law Review* 62 (1978): 1121-59.

31. *Davis v. Bandemer*, at 2810-2812.

32. Thernstrom, *Whose Votes Count?*

33. *Davis v. Bandemer* at 2811.

34. *Mobile v. Bolden*, 446 U.S. 55 (1980).

35. For details, see Grofman, "Alternatives to Single-member Plurality Districts"; Grofman, Migalski, and Noviello, "The Totality of Circumstances' Test"; Bernard Grofman, Michael Migalski, and Nicholas Noviello, "Effects of Multimember Districts on Black Representation in State Legislatures," *Review of Black Political Economy* 14, no. 4 (1986): 65-78; Kimball Brace,

Bernard Grofman, Lisa Handley, and Richard G. Niemi, "Minority Voting Equality: The 65 Percent Rule in Theory and Practice," *Law and Policy* 10, no. 1 (1988): 43-62.

36. Grofman, Migalski, and Noviello, "The 'Totality of Circumstances' Test."

37. Brischetto and Grofman, "Election System, the Voting Rights Act and Minority Representation."

38. Thernstrom, *Whose Votes Count?*

39. See Grofman, "Alternatives to Single-member Plurality Districts."

40. Brischetto and Grofman, "Election System, the Voting Rights Act and Minority Representation."

41. Thernstrom, "Voting Rights' Trap"; Thernstrom, *Whose Votes Count?* p. 172.

42. See, for example, Mack H. Jones, "The Voting Rights Act as an Intervention Strategy for Social Change: Symbolism or Substance?" in *The Voting Rights Act: Consequences and Implications,* ed. Lorn Foster (New York: Praeger, 1985).

43. See, for example, James Loewen, "Radically Polarized Voting in South Carolina" (paper presented to the American Political Science Association Meeting, Chicago, September 1987).

44. See, for example, *New York Times,* January 30, 1988, p. 14.

45. "2 Allege Politics Drive Census Decision," *Washington Post,* March 4, 1988.

46. Similar issues involving the 1985 Massachusetts State Census, used for mid-decade legislative reapportionment in that state, were litigated in federal district court in *Black Political Task Force et al. v. Connolly,* Civ. 87-1886 (Western Dist. Mass. 1988).

47. *Carey v. Klutznick,* 508 F.Supp. 420 (Southern Dist. N.Y. 1980).

48. 653 F.2d 732 (2d Cir. 1981).

49. 455 U.S. 999 (1982).

50. See Thomas M. Durbin, "A Constitutional and Legal Analysis of Adjustments of a Decennial Census by the Use of Sampling and Other Techniques," Congressional Research Service,

Library of Congress, Doc. 8754A, Washington, D.C., January 15, 1987.

51. "2 Allege Politics Drive Census Decision."

52. For example, in one case when I testified about the interpretation of registration and election statistics my testimony about levels of racially polarized voting was opposed by the chairmen of the statistics departments of two distinguished universities; however, they could not even agree between themselves as to what statistical procedure (if any) was appropriate.

53. For useful overviews, see Margo Anderson, "Planning the Future in the Context of the Past," *Society* 25 (March–April 1988): 39-48; and Frank O. Bean and Rodolfo O. de la Garza, "Illegal Aliens and Census Counts," *Society* 25 (March–April 1988): 48-53.

54. *Federation for American Immigration Reform (FAIR) v. Klutznick,* 486F. 564 (DCDC 1980).

55. *Ridge et al. v. Verity,* civ. no. 88-0351 (Western Dist. Pennsylvania 1988).

56. Bernard N. Grofman, "Criteria for Districting: A Social Science Perspective," *UCLA Law Review* 33, no. 1 (1985): 177-84, Table 3.

57. Gordon Baker and I have each proposed an approach based on an analogy to the "totality of circumstances" standard in the racial vote-dilution cases. See Gordon E. Baker, "Judicial Determination of Political Gerrymandering: 'A Totality of Circumstances' Approach," *Journal of Law and Policy* 3 (Winter 1986): 1-19; and Bernard N. Grofman, "Criteria for Districting."

58. This approach has been ably expounded by Charles Backstrom of the University of Minnesota and his colleagues. See Backstrom, Robins, and Eller, "Issues in Gerrymandering"; and Charles Backstrom, Leonard Robins, and Scott Eller, "Establishing a Statewide Electoral Effects Baseline," in *Political Gerrymandering and the Courts,* ed. Bernard Grofman (New York: Agathon Press, 1990).

59. See, for example, Richard G. Niemi and John Deegan Jr., "Competition, Responsiveness and the Swing Ratio," *American*

Political Science Review 72 (1978): 1304-23; Bernard N. Grofman, "Measures of Bias and Proportionality in Seats-Votes Relationships," *Political Methodology* 9 (1985): 295-327 also deals with this topic.

60. Bruce Cain, "Simple vs. Complex Criteria for Partisan Gerrymandering: A Comment on Niemi and Grofman," *UCLA Law Review* 33, no. 1 (1985).

61. This approach was pioneered in the study of racial gerrymandering independently by the political scientist Richard Engstrom (Richard L. Engstrom and John K. Wildgen, "Pruning Thorns from the Thicket: An Empirical Text of the Existence of Racial Gerrymandering," *Legislative Studies Quarterly* 2 [1977]: 465-79) and the political geographer John O'Loughlin (O'Loughlin, "Black Representation Growth and the Seat-Vote Relationship," *Social Science Quarterly* 60 [June 1979]: 72-86).

62. Grofman, "Measures of Bias and Proportionality"; Grofman, ed., *Political Gerrymandering and the Courts*; Samuel Kernell and Bernard Grofman, "Determining the Predictability of Partisan Voting Patterns in California Congressional Elections, 1978–1984," in ibid.

63. *Badham v. Eu*, slip opinion at p. 19.

64. The extent to which commissions actually improve districting plans from what the legislature might have otherwise enacted is a matter of considerable debate in the political science literature on redistricting.

65. In my view, "What defines a gerrymander is the fact that some group or groups (e.g., a given political party or a given racial/linguistic group) is discriminated against compared to one or more other groups in that a greater number of votes is needed for the former to achieve a given proportion of legislative seats than is true for the latter, and this bias is not one that can be attributed solely to the differing degree of geographic concentration among the groups" (Bernard Grofman and Howard Scarrow, "Current Issues in Reapportionment," *Law and Policy Quarterly* 4, no. 4 [1982]: 435-74). This is another way of saying that gerrymandering exists when votes are not accorded the same weight.

66. Bruce E. Cain and Janet C. Campagna, "Predicting Partisan Redistricting Disputes," *Legislative Studies Quarterly* 12, no. 2 (1987).

67. David R. Mayhew, "Congressional Representation: Theory and Practice in Drawing the Districts," in *Reapportionment in the 1970s*, ed. Nelson Polsby (Berkeley, Calif.: University of California Press, 1971).

68. Amihai Glazer, Bernard Grofman, and Marc Robbins, "Partisan and Incumbency Effects of 1970s Congressional Redistricting," *American Journal of Political Science* 31, no. 3 (1987): 680-701.

69. Cf. Thomas E. Mann, "Is the House of Representatives Unresponsive to Political Change?" in *Elections American Style*, ed. A. James Reichley (Washington, D.C.: Brookings Institution, 1987).

70. Grofman, "Criteria for Districting"; and Grofman, ed., *Political Gerrymandering and the Courts*.

71. *Reynolds v. Sims*, at 565-566.

72. For state legislative districting and local districting, the Supreme Court has been much more flexible, with a total deviation below 10 percent of "prima facie constitutional validity" for "legislatively enacted apportionments." *Connor v. Finch*, 431 U.S. 407 at 430-433 (1977). For further discussion see Grofman, "Criteria for Districting," pp. 79-84, 88-89.

SELECTED REFERENCES
ON 1990s REAPPORTIONMENT ISSUES

"American Census in 1990." Special minisymposium in *Society* 25 (1988): 39-60.

Auerbach, Carl A. "The Reapportionment Cases: One Person, One Vote—One Vote, One Value." In Philip Kurland, ed., *Supreme Court Review*. Chicago: University of Chicago Press, 1964, pp. 1-87.

Backstrom, Charles, Leonard Robins, and Scott Eller. "Establishing a Statewide Electoral Effects Baseline." In Bernard Grofman, ed., *Political Gerrymandering and the Courts*. New York: Agathon Press, 1990.

——. "Issues in Gerrymandering: An Exploratory Measure of Partisan Gerrymandering Applied to Minnesota." *Minnesota Law Review* 62 (1978): 1121-59.

Baker, Gordon, E. "Judicial Determination of Political Gerrymandering: 'A Totality of Circumstances' Approach." *Journal of Law and Policy* (Winter 1986): 1-19.

Brace, Kimball, Bernard Grofman, Lisa Handley, and Richard G. Niemi. "Minority Voting Equality: The 65 Percent Rule in Theory and Practice." *Law and Policy* 10, no. 1 (1988): 43-62.

Brischetto, Robert, and Richard Grofman. "Election System, the Voting Rights Act and Minority Representation in Texas

Cities and School Boards." Paper presented at the Annual Meeting of the American Political Science Association, Chicago, September 3-6, 1987.

Cain, Bruce. "Assessing the Partisan Effects of Redistricting." *American Political Science Review* 9, no. 2 (1985): 320-33.

―――. "Perspectives on *Davis v. Bandemer*: Views of the Practitioner, Theorist and Reformer." In B. Grofman, ed., *Political Gerrymandering and the Courts.* New York: Agathon Press, 1990.

―――. *The Reapportionment Puzzle.* Berkeley: University of California Press, 1984.

―――. "Simple vs. Complex Criteria for Partisan Gerrymandering: A Comment on Niemi and Grofman." *UCLA Law Review* 33, no. 1 (1985): 213-26.

――― and Janet C. Campagna. "Predicting Partisan Redistricting Disputes." *Legislative Studies Quarterly* 12, no. 2 (1987): 265-74.

Citro, Constance F., and Michael L. Cohen. *The Bicentennial Census: New Directions for Methodology in 1990.* Panel on Decennial Census Methodology, Committee on National Statistics, Commission on Behavioral and Social Sciences and Education, National Research Council. Washington, D.C.: National Academy Press, 1985.

Davidson, Chandler, and George Korbel. "At-Large Elections and Minority-Group Representation: A Re-Examination of Historical and Contemporary Evidence." *Journal of Politics* 43, no. 4 (1981): 983-1005.

―――. "At-Large Elections and Minority-Group Representation." In Chandler Davidson, ed., *Minority Vote Dilution.* Washington, D.C.: Howard University Press, 1984, pp. 65-81.

Dixon, Robert G., Jr. *Democratic Representations and Reapportionment in Law and Politics.* New York: Oxford University Press, 1968.

Durbin, Thomas M. "A Constitutional and Legal Analysis of Adjustments of a Decennial Census by the Use of Sampling and Other Statistical Methods." Washington, D.C.: Congressional Research Service, Library of Congress, Doc. 87-54A, January 15, 1987.

Engstrom, Richard L., and Michael D. McDonald. "The Election of Blacks to City Councils: Clarifying the Impact of Electoral Arrangements on the Seats/Population Relationship." *The American Political Science Review* 75, no. 2 (1981): 344-54.

———. "Quantitative Evidence in Vote Dilution Litigation, Part II: Minority Coalitions and Multivariate Analysis." *The Urban Lawyer* 19, no. 1 (Winter 1987): 65-75

———. "The Underrepresentation of Blacks on City Councils: Comparing the Structural and Socioeconomic Explanation for South/Non-South Differences." *Journal of Politics* 44 (1982): 1088-99.

——— and John K. Wildgen. "Pruning Thorns from the Thicket: An Empirical Test of the Existence of Racial Gerrymandering." *Legislative Studies Quarterly* 2 (1977): 465-79.

Glazer, Amihai, Bernard Grofman, and Marc Robbins. "Partisan and Incumbency Effects of 1970s Congressional Redistricting." *American Journal of Political Science* 31, no. 3 (1987): 680-701.

Grofman, Bernard. "Alternatives to Single-member Plurality Districts: Legal and Empirical Issues." *Policy Studies Journal* 9, special issue no. 3 (1982): 875-98. Reprinted in Bernard Grofman et al., eds., *Representation and Redistricting Issues.* Lexington, Mass.: Lexington Books, pp. 97-128.

———. "Criteria for Districting: A Social Science Perspective." *UCLA Law Review* 33, no. 1 (1985): 77-184.

———. Declarations in *Badham v. Eu* (excerpts). *PS* (Summer 1985): 544-49, 573-74.

———. "Measures of Bias and Proportionality in Seats-Votes Relationships." *Political Methodology* 9 (1983): 295-327.

———. "Toward a Coherent Theory of Gerrymandering: *Bandemer* and Thornburg." In ibid.

Grofman, Bernard, Michael Migalski, and Nicholas Noviello. "Effects of Multimember Districts on Black Representation in State Legislatures." *Review of Black Political Economy* 14, no. 4 (1986): 65-78.

———. "The 'Totality of Circumstances' Test in Section 2 of the Voting Rights Act: A Social Science Perspective." *Law and Policy* 7, no. 2 (1985): 209-23.

Grofman, Bernard, and Howard Scarrow. "Current Issues in Reapportionment." *Law and Policy Quarterly* 4, no, 4 (1982): 435-74.

Grofman, Bernard, ed. *Political Gerrymandering and the Courts.* New York: Agathon Press, 1990.

——— et al., eds., *Representation and Redistricting Issues.* Lexington, Mass.: Lexington Books, 1982.

Hardy, Leroy C. "Considering the Gerrymander." *Pepperdine Law Review* 4 (Spring 1977): 243-84.

Heilig, Peggy, and Robert J. Mundt. "Changes in Representational Equity: The Effect of Adopting Districts." *Social Science Quarterly* 64 (June 1983): 393-97.

————. "Do Districts Make a Difference?" *Urban Interest* (April 1981): 62-75.

Jones, Mack H. "The Voting Rights Act as an Intervention Strategy for Social Change: Symbolism or Substance?" In Lorn Foster, ed., *The Voting Rights Act: Consequences and Implications.* New York: Praeger, 1985, pp. 163-84.

Karlan, Pamela, and Peyton McCrary. Book Review: "Without Fear and Without Research: Abigail Thernstrom on the Voting Rights Act," *Journal of Law and Politics* 4, no. 4 (Spring 1988): 751-77.

Kernell, Samuel, and Bernard Grofman. "Determining the Predictability of Partisan Voting Patterns in California Congressional Elections, 1978-1984." In B. Grofman, ed., *Political Gerrymandering and the Courts.* New York: Agathon Press, 1990.

Kousser, J. Morgan. "The Undermining of the First Reconstruction." In Chandler Davidson, ed., *Minority Vote Dilution.* (Washington, D.C.: Howard University Press, 1984, pp. 27-46.

Lawson, Steven F. *In Pursuit of Power: Southern Blacks and Electoral Politics, 1965-1982.* New York: Columbia University Press, 1985.

Loewen, James. "Radically Polarized Voting in South Carolina." Paper presented at the American Political Science Association Meeting, September 1987.

Mann, Thomas E., "Is the House of Representatives Unresponsive to Political Change?" In A. James Reichley, ed., *Elections American Style.* Washington, D.C.: Brookings Institution, 1987.

Mayhew, David R. "Congressional Representation: Theory and

Practice in Drawing the Districts." In Nelson Polsby, ed., *Reapportionment in the 1970s*. Berkeley, Calif.: University of California Press, 1971.

Minisymposium. "Political Gerrymandering: *Badham v. Eu*, Political Science Goes to Court." In *PS* (Summer 1985).

Morrill, Richard. "Redistricting, Region, and Representation." *Political Geography Quarterly* 6 (1987): 241-60.

Niemi, Richard G., and John Deegan, Jr. "Competition, Responsiveness and the Swing Ratio." *American Political Science Review* 72 (1978): 1304-23.

O'Loughlin, John. "Black Representation Growth and the Seat-Vote Relationship." *Social Science Quarterly* 60 (June 1979): 72-86.

Polsby, Nelson, ed. *Reapportionment in the 1970s*. Berkeley, Calif.: University of California Press, 1971.

"Symposium: Gerrymandering and the Courts." *UCLA Law Review* 33, no. 1 (October 1985).

Thernstrom, Abigail. "The Odd Evolution of the Voting Rights Act." *The Public Interest*, no. 55 (Spring 1979): 49-76.

———. "Voting Rights' Trap." *The New Republic* 193, no. 10 (1985): 21-23.

———. *Whose Votes Count? Affirmative Action and Minority Voting Rights*. A Twentieth Century Fund Study. Cambridge, Mass: Harvard University Press, 1987.

Wells, David. "What Criteria Should Be Used in the Establishment of Legislative District Boundary Lines?" Paper presented at the National Conference on Government, Pittsburgh, Pennsylvania, November 16, 1981.

Williamson, Joel. *A Rage for Order: Black-White Relations in the American South since Emancipation.* London: Oxford University Press, 1986.

INDEX